AF545229

The Making Of a Preacher

By

Rev. George B. Kulp

ISBN 0-88019-203-8

Schmul Publishing Co., Inc.
Wesleyan Book Club
Salem, Ohio
1986

Printed by
Old Paths Tract Society Inc.
Shoals, Indiana 47581

CONTENTS

Chapter I

The Preacher's Call

Bishop Quayle, in his latest work, "The Pastor-Preacher," says, "If God or man has a manlier business than preaching, that business has not been set down in the list of masculine activities. Preaching is a robust business . . . . 'If, after the manner of men I have fought with the beasts of Ephesus' is not a phrase descriptive of physical or metaphysical lassitude or incapacity. The preacher is not a man of cartilage, he is a man of bone and sinew. He feels the riot of mighty deeds. Life is epic to him. 'I bear in my body the marks of the Lord Jesus' was another of the granitic sayings of Brother Paul, sometime preacher in the Church of God."

But let me say right here this preacher must be God's man—called of God to this business, saying, "This ONE thing I do"; "Woe is me if I preach not the Gospel"; conferring not with flesh and blood, but inquiring, "What wilt Thou have me to do?" and knowing by the Holy Ghost that he is a chosen vessel of God; the answer of the entire being is "Here am I; send me."

God alone can call a man to the ministry. This is a Divine prerogative. No sovereign would allow another to appoint his ministers. The Sovereign of the universe calls whom He will. Christ is the head of the Church, and He makes known to the Church that waits for guidance, whom He designates by the Holy Spirit. "Casting lots" or an apostle never was God's method. Jeroboam dared to make priests of others than Levites, and took of the lowest of the people for this high office, but it meant the doom of Israel and ruin for himself. No man taketh this honor unto himself but he that is called of God. Listen to the Word, "I have given your priest's office unto you as a service of gift, and the stranger that cometh nigh shall be put to death." "The prophet which shall presume to speak a word in my name, which I have not commanded him to speak, shall die." "Behold, I am against the prophets that steal my words." "Woe unto the foolish prophets, that have followed their own spirit, and have seen nothing." "The Holy Ghost said, Separate me Barnabas and Saul for the work WHEREUNTO I HAVE CALLED THEM." When God gave the plan of the Tabernacle to even the most minute detail, He also "called Bezaleel and filled him with the Spirit of God, in wisdom and understanding and in all manner of workmanship, to devise cunning work, to work in gold, and in silver, and in brass, and in cutting of stones, to set them, and in cutting of timber to work in all manner of workmanship," and it may be granted He would not have men to enter on the greatest work to which a mortal can be called, without the leading, inspiration and equipment of the Holy Spirit.

The Church of God, in all generations, has recognized this great truth. Luther, the moving spirit under God in the great Reformation, solemnly warns men, whatever their attainment in learning and wisdom, never to enter the ministry unless called of God. Vinet says: "We MUST be called of God. Whether external or internal, the call ought to be Divine." The Church of England requires an affirmative answer to the solemn question, "Do you trust that you are inwardly moved by the Holy Ghost to take upon this office and ministration, to serve God for the promoting of His glory and the edifying of His people?" Burnet well says, "Certainly the answer that is made ought to be well considered, for if any says, 'I trust so,' that yet knows nothing of any such motive, and can give no account of it, he lies to the Holy Ghost, and makes the first approach to the altar with a lie in his mouth, and that not unto men, but unto God."

There will be a time come in the ministry of every preacher when he will be glad "that God put him in the ministry," that he did not seek the office, for with the knowledge that it was God who called him there will come the assurance that He who called will also equip, defend, accompany and energize his servant, rendering him effective wherever his lot may be cast. "To me is this grace GIVEN that I should preach among the Gentiles the unsearchable riches of Christ, having this treasure in earthen vessels, that the excellency of the power may be of God and not of men."

Let us consider for a little, what do we understand by "a call to the ministry" or the "Preacher's Call"? When God calls to the work that an archangel might covet, the man knows it, and feels it so strongly that he says, "Woe is me if I preach not the Gospel." There is a necessity laid upon him, a sense of moral constraint, a consciousness that, unless he minds God, the heaviest of all woes, the woe of a remorseful conscience, the woe of a spirit that has fallen from a height of glory that might have been its own forever, would fall upon him if he proved unfaithful to the call. God's will becomes his will, God's purpose becomes his purpose. The manifested love of God in his heart must be an impelling power leading his whole being into captivity to the one work, drawing forth every energy of his nature into a holy and joyous service. Accompanying this will be an intense desire for the work, a cheerful obedience to the will of God. There may be, because of the knowledge of unworthiness and unfitness, a shrinking from such an humble dependence on Him who saith, "My grace is sufficient." If there is not this earnest desire for the work, founded upon obedience to God, and a burning love for souls, the trials to be met with in the ministry will soon quench one's zeal. THE MINISTRY IS A LIFE WORK, THE LOVE OF IT MUST BE LIFELONG. The desire is not for honor, or leisure, or ease of office, or plaudits of folks, or opportunities for advancement, but for the work belonging to it, with the joys and sorrows, pains and pleasures, labors and comforts attending a conscientious discharge of its duties.

God equips for this service, therefore take heart. When Jeremiah was told that he was ordained of God to be a prophet, that burning flame said, "Ah, Lord God, I can not speak, for I am a child," but God gave him assurance of all needed strength and succor. When Jesus called "the tiger of Tarsus," he knew what difficulties he would have from his past life in his future labors, and He personally said to him, "Rise and stand upon thy feet, for I have appeared unto thee for this purpose, to MAKE THEE A MINISTER AND A WITNESS both of these things which thou hast seen, and those things in the which I will appear unto thee, delivering thee from the people and from the Gentiles, unto whom I now send thee, to open their eyes and to turn them from darkness to light, and from the power of Satan unto God, that they may receive forgiveness of sins, and inheritance among them which are sanctified by faith that is in me." Paul never forgot this interview. He quoted these words in his old age. They made him calm and firm before the mighty and cruel. But for them, he might have fallen at the very threshold, for, be it remembered, his sense of personal weakness and unworthiness never left him; rather, it seemed to grow upon him, and though looking unto Jesus he could shout, "I can do all things through Christ strengthening me," yet he writes, "I am less than the least of all saints," and still later he cries, "I am the chief of sinners."

Good men, men called of God, invariably shrink from the awful responsibilities of the ministry. When Philip Henry was ordained, he humbly wrote, "I did this day receive so much honor and work as I ever shall know what to do with. Lord Jesus, proportion supplies accordingly." The better men are fitted for this great work, the deeper is their sense of unfitness and unworthiness. Let this be laid down as a maxim, "Men who seek and demand ordination are unworthy of it."

A call to the ministry that is from God will also be accompanied by a sense of the dignity of the office. Paul said the ministry "is a good work." He honored his own calling. There is no human comforter like an able minister of the New Testament. There are no glories like those to which he points and invites. A keen writer says, "A poor country preacher fighting the devil in his parish, has nobler ideas than Alexander ever had." When a man voluntarily quits the ministry for any secular office, it is as if the king of a great people had laid aside his scepter for a contable's bauble. A high appreciation of the ministry will produce a hearty devotion to it, and keep one from dabbling in stocks, promoting doubtful enterprises, or making the office a stepping-stone to some more lucrative profession.

Another part of a call to the ministry is a desire and willingness on the part of the one called to study to show himself approved unto God, a workman that needeth not to be ashamed; to "give attendance unto reading," acquiring the necessary learning and power of explaining and enforcing the truth. If God can do without our wisdom, He can certainly do without our foolishness, and it is foolishness to think that a call to the ministry is the end—it is only the beginning. It means putting forth every energy that God has given us, that we may be polished shafts in His quiver for the accomplishment of His work. No man is called to teach what he does not know and cannot or will not learn. One of very limited knowledge of divine things may be called TO PREPARE for the great work of this holy calling. "Follow me and I will make you fishers of men." A minister called of God must have an experimental knowledge of saving truth, and an acquaintance with the truths of Scripture that only comes through intense mental application and study. It is "the words of the wise that are as goads."

God's ministers must indeed be harmless as doves, but they must also be wise as serpents. The truth must be spoken, and it must be SPOKEN FITLY. Does that mean a college course? Not always. It may be "Brush College," or burning midnight oil, or "studying between times," but be sure of this, IT MEANS STUDY, and God's man always wants to be at his best. One preacher beginning his study for the ministry walked all the way to college, and slept out of doors on the ground for lack of money to pay for lodgings. Another blacked boots, swept corridors, and was a man of all work. Where there is a will there is a way—and YOU may find it.

CHAPTER II

The Preacher's Education

The Apostle declares we are to speak to men to their edification and comfort. While it is true that none but God can make a minister of the Gospel, it is true also that study and application and culture will make him an effective minister. We are not discounting the Holy Spirit—without Him the man educated at the feet of Gamaliel would have been a complete failure; He alone can give true spiritual views of God and life everlasting. A man who is rightly instructed as a servant of God will put a high estimation on the work of the ministry, and will use every lawful means to fit himself for his holy calling. Under the old dispensation, a thorough knowledge of God's will was enjoined upon all religious teachers. The true object of learning is to make truth plain, and in order to profit, learning must be sound—along right lines. The great American humorist said, "It is better not to know so much, than to know so much that isn't true." There cannot be too much SANCTIFIED learning. I trust that Holiness preachers, and all others, will learn the truth made manifest by so many complete failures all around us—God does not communicate necessary learning to ministers otherwise than by the Divine blessing upon the use of the ordinary means such as HEARING, READING, INQUIRY, STUDY AND REFLECTION. The apostles may have been ignorant men when called to follow Christ, but they were not so when they went forth to preach the Gospel in His name. They enjoyed His private and public instruction for three years in all, and in addition they had gifts of tongues, gifts of healing and revelations.

A preacher should be diligent in the use of the means. The man who is not industrious will not be effective. An idle, lazy man is a disgrace to the calling. A man of God should have no idle moments. Every day in one's life is a leaf in one's history. We must put into our treasury things new and old if we would have something to set before folks when they come. This cannot be acquired in a day; learning comes in a slow but regular process of accretion. Real knowledge, like everything else of the highest value, is not to be obtained easily. It must be worked for, studied for, thought for and prayed for. A liberal education will develop the whole mental system of the preacher, make his speculative inferences coincide with his practical convictions, and enable him to render a reason for the hope that is within him. Addison very beautifully says, "A statue lies hid in a block of marble; the art of the statuary only clears away the superfluous matter, removes the rubbish. The figure is in the stone, the sculptor only finds it." What sculpture is to a block of marble, education is to a human soul. The philosopher, the saint or the hero; the wise, the good, or the great man, very often lies hid in the plebeian, which a proper education might have disinterred, and have brought to light.

Such a course of study should be pursued as will enlarge and train the mind and enable one to communicate his thoughts in a proper manner. A good knowledge of our own tongue is a great attainment. I have known young men going to the foreign country where they must acquire the language of the people to whom they minister, who murdered the king's English, and apparently were unable to construct a sentence grammatically. In these days of good common schools such lamentable ignorance and neglect of opportunities is almost inexcusable.

The great object of a good education is to train the faculties to just and accurate thinking, investigation and statement, and to prepare them to acquire and use knowledge. Having acquired such a preliminary education as was attainable, let the preacher bring his mind to the study of all those things belonging to a thorough course of theological study, and store his mind with the facts and principles of revealed truth, as taught by inspired men, and as illustrated in the history of the world and of the Church. Let him bend all his energies toward acquiring the art of rightly presenting the Word and persuading men to righteousness.

In this work, natural and acquired, intellectual and moral qualities strangely unite. South says, "I am confidently persuaded that there is no endowment, no natural gift whatever, with which the great Father of lights has furnished the mind of man, but may in its highest operations be sanctified, and rendered subservient to the work of the ministry. Real religion engages no man, particularly no minister, to be dull, to lounge, and to be indolent, but on the contrary, it stirs up all the active powers of the soul in designing and bringing about great and valuable ends." All knowledge should be to one end, making the student an able minister of the New Testament. All studies are subservient to the great work of ministering holy things to immortal souls. All powers and attainments should be laid under tribute to one great end of holding forth the Word of life. The imperial part of man is his will, and any man called of God to preach, and not over fifty years of age, regardless of all his lack of opportunities in the past, may WILL to acquire knowledge and succeed in the acquisition.

Let him study systematically, sacredly setting apart and observing certain hours of the day, applying his mental powers to the work in hand, and he will fit himself to be a workman that needeth not to be ashamed. Theodore Cuyler says, "In the morning study books, in the afternoon door-plates." This will make him a preacher-pastor and acceptable to his congregation. Without study, he will be acceptable nowhere. What more pitiable sight can one see than that of a man called to preach, sitting on a drygoods box in a corner store, discussing the weather, crops, politics, the latest fad, when he ought to be studying hard as a preparation for future effectiveness? He must be a scribe well instructed unto the kingdom of Heaven, bringing out things new and old, and he must "meditate on these things." Visitors must not be allowed to break in upon these hours. Orton said, "I have little company and acquaintance, but I have a numerous and excellent society of prophets and apostles, practical writers with whom I have lately been conversing." More than one eminent man has had a warning to visitors put upon the door of his study, calling on them to be short, just as professional men have their card, "This is my busy day."

How many hours should one study? Find out by practice what is best for you, and then stick to it. Two hours a day for the secular days of the year are equal to 104 days of study of six hours each. In that time, the record proves, it, "many a man has learned a language, mastered science, or quite changed his mental habits." The hardest studies should be taken up in the earliest part of the day, while the mind is fresh and the body rested, and lighter studies reserved for afternoons and evenings. The morning hours are by far the best for study. One thing more and this chapter closes. In study, earnest prayer is a great help to success. Philip Henry wrote upon a studying day (which implies that this eminent divine had studying days), "I forgot when I began, explicitly and expressly, to crave help from God, and the chariot wheels drove accordingly. Lord, forgive my omissions, and keep me in the way of duty." Another old divine wrote, "If God drop not down His assistance, we write with a pen that hath no ink. If any would need walk dependently upon God more than another, the minister is he." It was once said to a minister of Christ whose labors had been abundantly successful, "If you did not plow in your closet you would not reap in your pulpit." STUDY AND PRAY, PRAY AND STUDY.

Chapter III

Personal Piety

Dr. Portor affirmed, "Vigorous piety is never maintained without systematic attention to reading of the Scriptures and sacred prayer." The preceding chapter takes it for granted that the man called of God to preach studies and prays, prays and studies. In so doing, he is becoming established, rooted and grounded, sinking down into God. Prayer will make the preacher a man of piety, and piety will make him a man of prayer. People have a right to expect more than ordinary piety in a minister of the Gospel, because he is a representative of Jesus Christ and should be "an ensample to the flock." The great object of preaching the Gospel is to form godly character, and therefore the preacher himself should strive to exhibit a character of the highest possible type. The Apostles were not only preachers, they were witnesses, having in themselves an experimental knowledge of the power of the Gospel they preached. A hearer once remarked, "My pastor's discourses are not brilliant, but his daily life is a sermon all the week." The "living epistle" is as eloquent and convincing as any words that may be uttered. It exemplifies the sermon. "Like priest, like people."

John Wesley said in one of his Conferences, "Why are not the people more holy? Because we are not more holy." If the standard is lower today than formerly, it is because the pulpit has lowered it. As vital piety decreases in the occupant of the pulpit, the utterances will be uncertain. Paul, whose logic was set on fire of the Holy Ghost, wrote to Timothy, "Keep thyself pure," "Let no man despise thee." Be true to all convictions founded upon God's Word and live what you preach. This implies that the preacher is to be like his message. If so, then he must obey the injunction, "Keep thy heart with all diligence, for out of it are the issues of life." The heart life hid with Christ in God insures the integrity of the outward life. THE GREATER YOUR PIETY THE GREATER WILL BE YOUR POWER. Scholarship, eloquence, great sermons, so called, are no substitutes for holiness of heart and life. The deeper you live in the heart of Christ, the deeper will you go into the hearts of your hearers. An ordinary man becomes extraordinary when he is a temple of the Holy Ghost. Bishop Quayle says, "The preacher must be like Christ all the day long, and all the night through. He must be a rock. He must be a voice. He must be a torch. Always going about doing good, always wanting to be a helper of mankind, always wanting to know things from God to tell man." To do this he must keep in communion with the Infinite One.

A man of God, called to preach, and keeping step with God, which implies walking with Him, will be led to preach much to his own soul. In so doing he will save himself and be enabled to win others. Melancthon said, "I feel sure that I have not otherwise handled theology than that I might derive profit myself. Another said, "I have prayed, I have talked, I have preached, but now I should perish if I did not feed on the bread I have broken to others." Henry Martyn wrote, "My first great business on earth is the sanctification of my own soul." Vinet adds, "Our first business is to be our own pastors," and every true preacher knows before we preach a sermon to others we derive good from it ourselves. We must not only commend holiness, but WE must practice it.

The unction that attends the ministry comes from being "apart often with God." Living piety prays and plans, weeps and rejoices, looking for the extension of Christ's kingdom and His glorious appearance. Rutherford, that sweet saint of old Scotland, assured his flock they were the object of his tears, cares, fears and daily prayers, and "My witness is above that your heaven would be two heavens for me, and the salvation of you all as two salvations to me." Alleine, the author of the "Alarm to the Unconverted," was infinitely and insatiably greedy of the conversion of souls, and to this end "he poured out his very heart." Doddridge, writing to a friend, remarked, "I long for the conversion of souls more sensibly than anything beside. I think I could not only labor but die for it with pleasure." President Edwards wrote, "My heart has been much on the advancement of Christ's kingdom in the world; the histories of the advancement of His kingdom in the past have been much to me. When I have read histories of past ages, the pleasant thing in all my reading has been to read of the kingdom of Christ being promoted." Men without piety never felt, or thought, or planned, as these men did.

The energies of the minister of the Gospel should be spent on things having connection with his work. An idle life, or an easy life is to be deplored. How can a man of God "take things easy," when all around him are thousands of blood-bought souls who are going rapidly toward eternal ruin, and more heathen are being born into the world every year than there are converts to Christianity from among them? Real genuine piety will beget and foster a generous love for perishing men, without which the most sacred duties will be dull, and seem a task instead of a delight. Blessed is he who is joyfully ready to spend and be spent for Christ and perishing men.

Chapter IV

The Earnest Preacher

Earnestness in the pulpit is so rare in these days that an earnest preacher excites remark, and is a subject of criticism. Men can be earnest in every other profession and command favor, but the minister of the Gospel must be calm and precise. Theodore Cuyler was a popular pastor in a leading denomination, and so earnest in his delivery of the messages and so intent upon winning souls, that critics remarked, "As he flings his arms and gesticulates, he makes one think of an old-fashioned Methodist exhorter." But where will we find men who did more effective work for God than these same old-fashioned Methodist preachers? Cuyler says, "The preaching of the Gospel is spiritual gunnery." When the old Methodist preacher went gunning he went "loaded for bear." He "aimed" to hit something, to arouse the indifferent, to warn the careless, to rebuke the faithless professor, as well as comfort the sorrowing, strengthen the weak, and edify believers. Many an ordinary discourse has produced an extraordinary effect by an intensely earnest delivery, and it is equally true that many an excellent discourse has failed to produce any impression on account of the dull and motionless manner of the speaker. If the preacher does not "warm up," he may be sure his congregation will not be warmed under his preaching. One of the Christian philanthropists of New York City died a few weeks ago. He was a cultured business man, a constant attendant upon the Sabbath services and the prayer meetings, and Dr. Buckley said of him in an editorial in the "Christian Advocate," "He liked sermons that instructed him and aroused his emotions."

The preacher whose soul is red hot with a holy love of Jesus and dying souls will arouse his hearers, and if he does not succeed in moving them toward a better life, his effort is a failure. The earnestness of purpose of the fiery Paul, apostle to the Gentiles, is marked in emphatic declaration, "This one thing I do," and is seen in his addresses, leading his hearers to say, "Thou art beside thyself; much learning hath made thee mad." Rowland Hill said, "Because I am in earnest men call me an enthusiast," but he lives today in the lives of hundreds of his spiritual children while his critics are forgotten. Charles Simeon kept the picture of Henry Martyn in his study. Move where he would throughout the apartment, it seemed to keep its eyes upon him, and ever to say to him, "Be in earnest, be in earnest," and the good Simeon would bow to the speaking picture and say, "Yes, I will be in earnest, I will. I will not trifle, for souls are perishing and Jesus is to be glorified." It was said of John Wesley, "In his preaching he had clearness, force and earnestness—the qualities that produce connection." When he preached in the prison at Bristol, men dropped on every side as thunderstruck, while God bore witness to His Word, and the convictions were so lasting that in the prison the corridors "rang with cries." Wesley exulted in these experiences. When the Word of the Lord is as fire in a man's bones, he will be in earnest, and the fire in his own soul will not only kindle his tongue but also the hearts of his hearers. The sermons of Frederick W. Robertson were models of clearness of thought and read well today, but they owed much of their power to the fact they were delivered "with a fiery glow." Where is the minister who has not seen his congregation marvelously moved under a sermon, but upon preaching that same sermon elsewhere, produced no impression whatever? Was not the difference in the preaching? Do not be afraid of earnestness when it is the result of the unction from the Holy One. Dr. Duff's eloquence would sweep his audience like a hurricane, yet an admirer says of him, "Such outlandish contortions of gestures as his I never witnessed before. A distinguished lawyer has said, "The two best qualities of a sermon are simplicity and earnestness," and he added, "If I had a student in my office, who was not more in earnest to win his first ten-dollar suit before a justice of the peace than some ministers seem to be in trying to save souls, I would kick such a student out of my office."

Downright earnestness to save souls "hides a multitude of sins" in all preachers. If a preacher is in earnest, has a passion for souls, makes their salvation his one object, his hearers will forgive many blunders and mistakes. Load your gun with uncompromising truth, take aim and FIRE, let God take care of results. Preach for souls, preach for eternity; the more soul you put into your preaching, the more souls you will win for Christ. Baxter preached while his heart burned within him, and while he was speaking a live coal from off the altar fired his sermon with seraphic fervor. He had a large mind, an active intellect, a melting heart, a kindling eye and a moving voice, and he called on all that was in him to aid him in his preaching. The only teacher that gave him lessons in action and attitude was feeling, real, genuine, holy feeling; and this taught him how to look, how to move, how to speak. He believed with Paul that "it is a good thing to be zealously affected always," and consequently that earnest, fervid preaching is truly apostolic. Two lines Baxter wrote reveal the preacher:

"I'll preach as tho' I ne'er should preach again,
And as a dying man to dying men.

Ryle says of him, "He always spake like one who saw God and felt death at his back." George Whitfield was a burning example of the earnest minister. He had preached 18,000 times, though he died at the age of fifty-six. He lived to win souls for Christ. He made everything bend to that one great purpose. He was not in the same class with John Wesley, had neither the depth nor the knowledge, yet he was the greater preacher. He was something that brings to mind the Word: "His ministers a flaming fire." He lived, he prayed, he read, he wept, he rejoiced to accomplish this one great purpose of his life. How few ministers preach with all their might, or speak about everlasting joy or torment in such a manner as to make men believe they are in good earnest! The blow falls so lightly that hard-hearted sinners do not feel it.

People do not need to have their heads stoved so much as to have their hearts touched, and they stand in the greatest need of that sort of preaching which has the greatest tendency to do this. An earnest heart in the preacher will produce an earnest manner, and as he sows so shall he reap. How can a man be earnest for souls, and overlook the invitation to the convicted sinner? Are camp meetings and revival services the only time for reaping? We have heard men preach sermons that stirred the hearers, and have seen them sit down, without an altar call. The one object of the Gospel is to get men to God. "He that converteth a sinner from the error of his ways saveth a soul from death and shall cover a multitude of sins." If but one soul responds, it will set all the joybells of Heaven ringing and make the heart of God glad. The earnest preacher will be a SOUL-WINNER.

Chapter V

The Revival Preacher

"He that winneth souls is wise" and "He that is wise winneth souls." The one object of the man called of God to preach is to win souls; all his preaching tends to this one end. If he preaches to the Church it is to instruct, confirm, establish, that it may be effective in the work for which God established it. The increase in the membership of the Church should, and will if it is of God, increase its power. The first disciple of Jesus went out and brought another; the third went and brought in the fourth. A revival was on hand immediately. The Church of God today needs the revival preacher, and no other makes full proof of his ministry. "Whosoever shall call on the name of the Lord shall be saved. How then shall they call on him in whom they have not believed? and how shall they believe in him of whom they have not heard? and how shall they hear without a preacher? and how shall they preach except they be sent?" (Rom. 10:13-15). Here the salvation of souls and the preaching of the Gospel are forever united by the Holy Ghost. "What God hath joined together let no man put asunder." "As the Father hath sent me, even so have I sent you." "The Son of man came to seek and to save the lost." The Spirit and the Church and the individual believer all unite in saying, "Come." All Heaven is interested in sinners getting back to God. There is joy in the presence of God among the angels over one sinner that repenteth. What engages the interest and effort of Heaven ought to engage the interest and effort of the church on earth; the Church triumphant and the Church militant are one.

"One army of the living God
Before His throne they bow;
Part of the host have crossed the flood
And part are crossing now."

Revivals are the necessity of the Church. Without them, it will cease to exist. Revival preachers are a necessity. There are preachers, men of reputation too, that never once in all their lives distinctly concentrated their efforts to the single purpose of converting men. Their efforts are to finish an eloquent sermon, to develop theological or biblical truth, to thrill aesthetically an audience, to spread a popular fame, to gather crowds, to build a large church. These have their reward, success in their objects. But here is a lonesome preacher, faithful to his calling, by prayer, by fasting, by waiting on God, by study of the Word, by humble dependence on the Holy Ghost aiming to win men for God, and he does it; he honors God and God honors him. Jacob Knapp, laboring in New York, in a meeting when the devil put up great resistance, said publicly, "My bones bleach in Penn Yann, or I see the work of the Lord prosper." Of course a revival began, and began at once; that night people ran to the altar. The preacher who pays the price will enkindle the faith and prayers and enthusiasm of others.

If we would have extensive and powerful revivals of religion, we must have a good estimate of their value, remembering, in the first place, that the Holy Spirit, the Executive of the Godhead, is the sole Author of genuine revivals. He is the true oil of gladness; when He blows on the garden the spices will flow out. Nothing that man can do is a substitute for His presence. The preacher, without the Holy Ghost, is as dead as the branch in which there is no sap. The Church, without Him, is as dry and barren as the fields without heaven's dew and rain. If the Spirit of God does not aid, our hearts fail us while longing for much valued blessings.

The revival preacher preaches the Word of God, remembering that his Master said, "The Spirit of the Lord God is upon me, because he hath anointed me to preach the gospel." He enjoined His disciples to do as He had done. He has set them as watchmen, they must give the alarm. He has given them the trumpet, they must blow until the gladsome sound is heard. His object and theirs is the same—"to open the eyes of the blind, to turn them from darkness to light, and from Satan unto God, that they may receive forgiveness of sins, and inheritance among them which are sanctified by faith that is in Christ Jesus," to turn men from sin unto holiness. He not only preaches the Word, he preaches it boldly, without fear or favor, yet preaches it in love, his heart bathed in tears. Spurgeon said of Paul, "He was the kind of preacher whom you would expect to see walk down the pulpit stairs straight into the coffin and then stand before his God ready for his last account." Why not so of every preacher? Preaching for eternity, the blood-bought souls, over whom Christ wept, why not? "Judgment will I lay to the line, and righteousness to the plummet, and the hail shall sweep away the refuge of lies, the water shall overflow the hiding-place, and your covenant with death shall be disannulled, and your agreement with Hell shall not stand."

God's Word, His message for the preacher, to the unsaved, unpenitent hearer before him, prevents, will not allow, of any law or cold standard of indifference. We must preach the Word; preach not what people want to hear, but what they ought to hear. Woe be to him who willingly keeps back any part of the counsel of God! "Preach the preaching that I bid thee preach." This means surely, he must unfold doctrines and enforce duties, must present promises and pronounce threatenings, must hold forth encouragement without concealing responsibilities; must preach the law and the Gospel distinctly; yet he must not forget that mercy triumphs over judgment, and that where sin abounded, grace does much more abound. As a physician of souls, he must know and declare the extent of the malady, no less than the perfection of the remedy. As men are poor, let him show them the riches of divine grace. As men are dead in trespasses and sins, let him point them to Him who is the life of the world. As they are naked, let him tell of the Lord our righteousness. As they are vile, let him show how Christ is made unto us sanctification. In short, let him preach the whole truth of the Scripture. "The prophet that hath a dream let him tell a dream, but he that hath my word, let him speak my word faithfully. What is the chaff to the wheat? saith the Lord. Is not my word like as a fire, saith the Lord, and like a hammer that breaketh the rock in pieces?" This kind of preaching will not make the preacher popular, but nevertheless he will be in demand. There will be hungry hearts crying out to know the way, to be delivered from the burden of sin, and while the God-given message will bring the sinner to Sinai where rolling thunders and lightning flashes will make him fear and tremble, yet, if he "follows on to know," he will also be brought to Calvary where he will lose his burdens and be enabled to say,

> *"Thus far did I come laden with my sin,*
> *Nor could aught ease the grief that I was in,*
> *Till I came hither; what a place is this?*
> *Must here be the beginning of my bliss?*
> *Must here the burden fall from off my back?*
> *Must here the strings that bind it to me crack?*
> *Blest cross; blest sepulchre! blest rather be*
> *The Man that there was put to shame for me!"*

That great revival preacher Whitfield often said, "Would ministers preach for eternity, they would act the part of true Christian orators, for then they would endeavor to move the affections and warm the heart, and not constrain their hearers to suspect they dealt in false commerce of unfelt truth." There is a Heaven and there is a Hell. Let the preacher duly speak of both. The Word of God teaches us all we must believe, practice, and experience in order to salvation. It is the Word of life. It is the doctrine according to godliness that is able to make men wise unto salvation.

The revival preacher preaches the whole Gospel and preaches it AS becomes a man sent of God. This little adverb leads us to the manner of preaching. Someone may say, "Is it necessary to say anything of the manner?" One with any experience would think so. The Archbishop of Canterbury said to Garrick, "Pray inform me how it is that you gentlemen of the stage can effect your auditory with things imaginary as if they were real, while we of the Church speak of things real, which many of our congregation receive as imaginary?" "The reason is plain," said Garrick, "we actors speak of things imaginary as though they were real, while too many in the pulpit speak of things real as if they were imaginary." He who speaks of God, eternity, sin, salvation, death, judgment, Heaven and Hell, should speak as becomes an ambassador of Heaven bearing a message to dying men and women, Hell bound without Christ, yet who may become sons of God without rebuke.

It must be serious preaching that will make men serious in hearing and obeying it. We are dealing in eternal verities. Heaven is not a dream; Hell is not the vagary of disordered imagination; damnation is not fiction. It is a solemn thing to die, it is a solemn thing to live. It is an awfully solemn thing to preach to candidates for Eternity. He who "woos a smile" when he should "win a soul" is a clown, not a preacher, such as God's man should be.

The preacher aiming for the glory of God should preach in plain English. I have been amused at men whose early advantages were limited, as they gave Hebrew and Greek, acquired not through culture, but a concordance, while educated hearers smiled at their pronunciation, and their revelation of weakness. Baxter said if people had sinned in Latin, he would have written his "Reformed Pastor" in Latin, but as they had sinned in English, he must also write in English. Romaine was required by some of his hearers to display a little more learning in the pulpit. His very next opportunity he read his text in Hebrew, saying, "I suppose scarcely anyone in the congregation understands that." He then read it in Greek, and added, "There may be one or two understand me now. I will now read it in Latin." He did so, and said, "Possibly a few more comprehend me." Last of all he repeated the text in English, and said, "There now, you all understand it. Which do you think is best? I hope always to preach that the most ignorant person in the congregation may understand me." Aim to give men the truth, show the people their sins, not your eloquence or learning. "That is not the best looking-glass which is most guilded, but which shows the truest face." Luther said, "To preach simply is high art. Christ does it Himself. He speaks of husbandry, of sowing seed, and uses peasant similes." The old bishop was right when he said, "Brethren, it will take all our learning to make things plain."

The revival preacher will preach to the consciences of men, and the preaching should be direct. Peter's sermon on the Day of Pentecost was a model in this respect. How it bore down on the conscience of every man! Such preaching God blesses. "Ye have taken and by wicked hands crucified and slain." Conscience was on the side of the speaker, and the appeal had a visible effect which could not be concealed. We need today preaching that will convince and move men to act from force of truth. Men cannot extinguish their conscience even by false principles, or by their creed. Herod was a Sadducee, did not believe in angel, or spirit, or resurrection, but when he heard of the mighty works of Jesus, he said, "it is John whom I beheaded." His principles fled before the power of conscience. Direct preaching to the conscience of men impels to action. Here the Methodist exhorters were "at home." They pushed men to action. Moody and Harrison and Sam Jones were especially effective because they were direct in their appeals and urged to action at once, pointing out the peril of delay. God uses the gift of urgent appeal; directness always has force, and produces results.

Chapter VI

The Man in the Pulpit

It may seem rather strange that after the preceding chapters we should take such a caption as the above, but we believe there is a demand for MANLY men and WOMANLY women. We have no more use for the effeminate man than we have for masculine women. The Amazons of Africa have always to us appeared out of place, and we still think so, though the suffragets of today declare they are willing to enroll at the country's call. The man in the pulpit should be so God-centered he will lose sight of himself. I have heard men preach and all the time thought of and saw the men, they were self-centered, with an air of "I am doing this"; the message was in the background. I think it was Rowland Hill who saw an auctioneer selling off a picture. He was behind it, expatiating upon the merits of the picture. The picture was in full view, but he was out of sight. "That," said Hill, "is the way I want to preach, so Christ only will be seen." Let the man be lost in the message. It is not the spoon that nourishes the invalid, but what the spoon carries. It is not the preacher that blesses the hearer, but the message that the preacher brings. A preacher must be a positive man; that is, must have a positive religious experience. Roberts says, "Ministers who are lacking in religious experience not only cannot build up others in a faith and holiness which they do not possess, but they will be likely to bring down to their own level those under their care who have a deeper experience than themselves, or, failing in this, to persecute and oppose them. Godless ministers are the real cause of the decline in the Church of spirituality. The purest light shining through a colored medium becomes colored. Worldly, time-serving preachers promote a worldly religion. They may multiply converts, but their converts mold the Church more than the Church molds them."

A positive religious experience will produce positive preaching. The compromising preacher may have more joiners, but the positive preacher will get more people to Christ. Ever since Constantine took the Church up into a high mountain and showed it the kingdoms of the world, seducing it from allegiance to its lawful Head, the Church has had the favor of the State, but has lost its power. What Almighty God put asunder man should never join together. It is high time for a divorce, and positive preaching by a positive man with a positive religious experience, will aid much in bringing it about.

The preacher should have a standard such as a positive religious experience will give, and this standard he will preach, and he should examine himself to see if he abides in the faith. Bishop Hedding said in an address to the Conference, " 'Examine yourselves whether ye be in the faith,' is an admonition necessary for ministers as well as for people. Men are liable to be deceived in regard to their own conversion, and to satisfy themselves with a work of the imagination instead of the work of the Spirit. Let us therefore compare our experiences with the Word of God and satisfy ourselves that we are really born of the Spirit." "We are in danger of being deceived in another way. Having been really born of God, we may backslide in heart, lose the spirit we received from Heaven, and yet retain the form, the morals, and the profession of Christianity, and still persuade ourselves we are as pious as when in the first love. Let us look into this matter and see whether we are indeed as near to Christ as when we were first made partakers of His love. We ought to be nearer. We should be growing in grace and in the knowledge of our Lord Jesus Christ."

Unless we examine ourselves frequently, we will be in great danger of lowering the standard below that of the Bible. We say the standard of the Bible, for the Church is way below the standard, and the positive preacher is needed because he must combat the present state of the Church, and in so doing he will surely arouse the carnal and unsaved. President Finney says, "Until we put away from the minds of men the common error that the current Christianity of the Church is the true Christianity, we can make but little progress in converting the world. For, in the first place, we cannot save the Church itself from the bondage to the world in this life, nor from the direct doom of the hypocrite in the next. For this religion of the mass of nominal professors does not answer the descriptions given of true piety in the Word of God." Mark you, this is from a man of God, a positive preacher, who held meetings extensively all over the country and was acquainted with the most spiritual of the churches, and since his time there has been a great decline in piety. Finney holds most emphatically that the Church standard is low. Will it not require, then, a positive man to face such a condition? Mr. Finney was not alone in this view of the Church. Bishop Foster, of the M. E. Church, said in a public address, and we give it just as reported: "Just now four out of five with their names on the Church roll are doing nothing—almost absolutely nothing. Four out of five contribute but little to the treasury of the Church benevolences, and four out of five do nothing in the line of personal work for Christ. They go to church perhaps once on each Sabbath, if the weather is not inauspicious, and when the next Sunday comes, and the conditions are the same, they go again, and so on through the weeks and months and years, and God's blessed cause is not made one whit stronger in membership or influence for their living." Bishop Peck confirms these statements, and says, "There is a general impression that many members are not useful, not holy in life, not worthy representatives of practical Christianity, really a burden and not a help to the Church. But the extent of the sad fact is not seen, that the cold, worldly or indifferent in our midst are really a large majority, and that the Church it compelled to bear the reproach of a vast multitude of sinful men. Nor is the peril of these brethren fully appreciated. It comes to be considered so much a matter of course that the evil is looked upon as irremediable, and the few to go on to bear the burdens, and do the work which belongs to the many, and charity becomes indifference. Discipline is rare and finally impossible. Let me say distinctly, but with tender concern, that this represents a fact so large as to explain, to a great extent, our failure in Church reforms and Christian power, and calls for the most rousing, pathetic, and persistent appeals from the pulpit and press." With these facts, substantiated by spiritual men in the Church everywhere, is there not a crying demand for positive men, with positive experiences, preaching persistently the whole Gospel, crying unto ZION, 'awake and sin not'?"

Some time ago, a leading divine in one of our large denominations said, "You know very well half of the members in the churches are not converted." Will anything less than positive preaching, backed by the Holy Ghost, ever produce a better condition, or lead to a better state of affairs? It is incumbent upon the man in the pulpit "to cry aloud and spare not"; to lift up his voice like a trumpet and show the professed Church of God its transgressions and the house of Jacob its sins. The Church today is dying because of the weak pabulum it receives from the invalids in the pulpit, and rugged Christian characters under such ministration are surely impossible.

A positive man with a positive knowledge of the power of the Gospel in his own life will "speak as one having authority," and sure of his position. "He is God's man sent to preach to God's other men," bearing the message he was ordained from before the foundation of the world to deliver, and having this assurance, how can he do anything else but give it, without any qualification, but, on the contrary, rejoicing in being honored of God to speak for Him, to the dying and unsaved all around him? The gnashing of teeth, black looks, unkind criticisms, will not affect him. Praying at him will not stir him. He is so yoked up with God and centered in Him, he prances in his soul, whenever he has the privilege of preaching the Gospsel, of carrying the King's message. He says "Amen!" to all the will of God and wins souls that they may be stars in the crown of Jesus his Master and Lord. Such men are needed and will be a success everywhere. Like their Master, they "cannot be hid"; they will not have to seek places, places will seek them. They will have a holy independence that God will bless, for it is founded upon a conscious dependence upon Him. May the tribe of positive, manly men, Christ-men, increase, and may the day hasten when we will be rid of the namby-pamby mugwumps who adorn (???) the profession for the bread and butter that comes with it, and, dealing "in milk and mildness," neither please God nor offend the devil. Amen!

Chapter VII

The Growing of Sermons

Someone has said, "Poets are born, not made." Talmage said in one of his sermons, "Church sextons are born, not made." There is truth perhaps in both statements, but we KNOW sermons "grow, they are not made." The man who is called to preach has a message, and he knows it. His message the theologians call a sermon. It must be of God and founded upon the Word of God; in other words, it must be Scriptural. The Apostles were not only preachers, they were witnesses. "That which we have seen and heard declare we unto you." The tongue's holiest mission is to proclaim the Christ of whom we have an experimental knowledge. "We KNOW whom we have believed"; "we preach not ourselves but Christ Jesus the Lord." To be an ambassador for the Lord Jesus Christ is the noblest vocation to which angels or men ever have been called. An ambassador bears the King's message, the counsels of God once delivered to the saints. As a student of the Word of God, he will constantly be receiving inspiration from the Word. Texts, messages, will flash before him, his mind will seize upon them, measure them, investigate them, enlarge upon them. Some precious truth from Calvary will be as tender as a mother's caressing speech, or if from Sinai, it will trumpet in thunder tones; again, it will glow with the glory akin to that on Tabor's summit, or manifest itself in tears and sobs over a perishing world. As God's man, with a message to the people for whom He gave His Son, thinks upon themes for eternity, they will be marvelously magnified by the Holy Spirit, and be as fire in his bones until he delivers them, for he is to preach "the things angels desired to look into." The preacher who is God's man will have a sermon, not a lecture, if he studies the Word, and a careful study of the Word will make him a doctrinal preacher. He who "spake as a man never spake," to whom was given the tongue of the learned, who could say, "The Spirit of the Lord God is upon me, because he hath anointed me to preach," dealt in doctrine. Meeting Nicodemus, He preached to him of human guilt, the Atonement, regeneration, divine love in redemption, the need of faith and the promise of Heaven. Paul revelled in great doctrinal themes, giving us in one book, the Epistle to the Romans, what Coleridge pronounced the profoundest book in existence. Finney, a prince among evangelists, "bombarded the consciences of sinners with a tremendous broadside of doctrine." Cuyler says, "Merely hortatory sermons seldom amount to much. You must tell your hearers what to believe and what to do, before you urge them to do it."

God in His Word gave law, then repentance, threatens vengeance for sin, casts man down in his own sight, and lets him look even into Hell, with fear of conscience for his disobedience, but afterward He comforts him, raises him up and heals him. Men need law and Gospel today, but law first. Sinai came before Calvary, and both precede Pentecost. Let them stay where God placed them and let us follow always the divine order.

Sermons grow? Surely Law proclaims the need of the Gospel; Sinai demonstrates there must be another mountain —a Calvary, and living witnesses to the power of the Blood must be energized by Pentecost. Genesis foreshadows all the doctrines that followed after, and without Revelation the Book would be incomplete. The one book grew to sixty-six. It heartens us who experienced "Paradise Lost," to know of "Paradise Regained"; no angel barring the way to the Tree of Life, but an invitation from the heart of God: "Whosoever will, let him come"—He who lost the right to the tree, may do His commandments, and have a right to the tree again, and enter in through the gates into the city.

Sermons will grow with experience. "If any man will do his will, he shall know (experience) the doctrine." Prove it true in his own heart and life, and as his experience widens and deepens, his sermons will take on breadth and depth. It had the force of a sneer when the wits of the days of early Methodism said of the preachers, "Having nothing else to preach, they inevitably fell back on their experience," but what a blessing to have an experience, an experimental knowledge of God's power and willingness to forgive sins, of the power of the Blood to cleanse from all sin, to be able to say in the Holy Ghost, "the Comforter has come." "Jesus sanctifies me NOW." Thank God where there is corn in the hopper you will surely get meal. When there is a treasury, the good man will have no trouble getting out things new and old. Where sermons do not grow, there is either shallowness, or laziness. The man who boasts he has not produced a new sermon for years is backslidden already and needs to go to the altar. If God calls men to preach, HE CAN ALSO RECALL THE CALL, and I can readily believe a lazy preacher has lost his call.

Soil that grows sermons will keep it up if well fertilized. What do I mean? simply this. One who keeps in touch with Heaven will have the vernacular of Heaven; keep in touch with Jesus and travail of soul for the lost will obtain; have the Spirit abiding within, and there will be an outgush of soul speech that will reach souls. Be conscious that you are God's man, called to tell His message to His men who need to hear more than they need all else beside, and that very consciousness will cause one to see "sermons in stones, books in rolling brooks and God in everything." Chalmers, riding with the driver on a stage coach one day, observed the Jehu use his long lash on the leader, and said to him, "What did you do that for?"and the answer was, "See that big stone ahead by the road side? That leader always shies when he gets there, so I gave him something else to think of." Chalmers went home with that thought, and out of it GREW that great sermon, "The Expulsive Power of a New Affection." Bunyan's "Pilgrim's Progress" grew. The author said so, and thus poetically expresses it:

"And thus it was, I writing of the way
And race of saints in this our glorious day,
Fell suddenly into an allegory
About their journey and the way to glory,
In more than twenty things which I set down.
This done, I twenty more had in my crown;
And they again began to multiply
Like sparks that from the coals of fire do fly."

"Out of the abundance of the heart the mouth speaketh," and where the heart is full there will be no trouble about the delivery. Do not be alarmed if you cannot memorize as some do. Find out God's method for you and follow that. Better a thousand times, "notes" and "outlines" than labored memorizing of an entire sermon, word by word. The example of many of our most useful ministers will be helpful if you study their methods. The admirers of Dr. Seiss would do to remember that this natural-born orator took the manuscript of his entire sermon into the pulpit with him, and Dr. James M. Buckley, of the "Christian Advocate," in an editorial after Dr. Seiss departed, said he was one of the most polished speakers he ever listened to, holding his audience during a long pastorate in Philadelphia. No one can deny his spirituality, ability, judgment or usefulness. John Fletcher, the sainted vicar of Madeley, of whom Wesley said, "He was the holiest man I ever knew," has left behind his notes upon many sermons. Charles Spurgeon, whose usefulness and ability were undoubted, left behind a wealth of "sermon notes" which his publishers and executors have issued. Charles Pitman, that prince of pulpit orators, used carefully written notes in his ministry and won thousands for Christ. Repetition of sentences laboriously acquired in memorizing hour after hour is not the manner of the true orator, is death to spontaneity, and checks the flow of language prompted by the Holy Spirit. I have seen men take a text, put the Bible to one side at once, and then proceed to deliver their carefully memorized sermon, word for word, and I have seen that which would excite ridicule, were it not so painful—men, just beginning to preach, supposing these brethren were speaking extempore, take a text, put the Bible to one side, and then, open their mouths, and begin. They were called of God, had in them material out of which preachers are made, but foolishly imitating others, they floundered and fell. Ezra stood upon a pulpit of wood, opened the Book in the sight of all the people and blessed the Lord. The book was honored, should be today. We are preachers of the Word; the Book is our authority; let us act what we profess. There is a method best adapted to each one, helpful to one's usefulness, and that God will honor. It will be natural to the speaker, leaving him unembarrassed and receptive, revelling in his privilege as an ambassador of God and speaking as one that has authority.

Chapter VIII

The Preacher as a Pastor

Paul in an address declared that he not only taught publicly but from "house to house." An uncouth, uncultured, hard-handed son of toil, who had found God in the pardon of sins, said he always enjoyed the sermon better if he had had a chance to shake the preacher's hand during the week. Theodore Cuyler, one of the best examples of the preacher-pastor the Church has produced in a century, remarks: "The work of every preacher is two-fold—partly in the pulpit and partly out of the pulpit. The two ought to be inseparable. What the providence of God and good common sense have joined, let no man put asunder." Labors outside of the pulpit occupy more or less time during every day of the week. The great business of a preacher is to win souls to Jesus Christ, and to build them up in godly living, and all this cannot be accomplished by two sermons a week, even if they were the best that Paul himself could deliver. In fact, the largest part of Paul's recorded work was quite other than public preaching. As for our Lord, He has left us but one extended discourse and a few shorter ones, but we have many narratives of His personal visits, personal conversations, and labors of love with the sick, the sinning, the suffering. He was the Shepherd who knew every sheep. Only a few men can be great preachers, but every minister who has a good heart and good sense can be a good pastor. Devote the forenoon of every day except Monday to your studies, and in the afternoon of five days in the week to pastoral visiting. Religiously observe Monday as your sabbatic rest day, remembering that He who sent Israel into captivity seventy years because they, for 490 years, deprived the land of its "seventh year sabbath," will not prolong your life if you violate His law, and abuse your body. The physical exercise in pastoral visiting will be a benefit, and the spiritual benefits will be tenfold more. Do not "loaf" in any home, especially if it's a fine one, but visit the poor and needy as well as those in influence. "Go not only where you are needed" but "where you are needed most." Always, night or day, visit the sick and dying. Spurgeon said once, "I have been today to visit two of my church-members who are near eternity, and both are as happy as if they were going to a wedding. Oh, it makes me preach like a lion when I see how my people can die!" Never spend your time in frivolous conversation or gossip. Talk about religious experience, personal relation to God, not with the air of a schoolmaster examining a pupil, but in the real spirit of the "Shepherd and Bishop of our souls."

In your visiting you can discover whether your preaching is going home, whether Gospel shot is striking. The officers on the battleships off Santiago were anxious to know how many shots "struck home," and they smiled at the almost fruitless shooting of the enemy. "Gunnery that hits no one is not worth the powder." Preaching in the Holy Ghost accomplishes something, and glorifies the Triune God. Help the weak, lead the penitent inquirer to Jesus, comfort those who place confidence in you and seeking your advice reveal their hearts unto you. Never violate the confidence reposed in you, but, as in Christ's stead, lend the helping hand to the needy. A home-visiting, hot-hearted preacher, with the real Spirit of Jesus, seeking to "walk even as He walked," will not have to bemoan empty pews. Having won the hearts of his people, the preacher can preach plainly and give no offence, and lead on up into Canaan.

Do not make long visits. John Wesley declared it hard to spend over thirty minutes profitably. "People do not need sitting up with unless they are sick." Learn to distinguish between social visiting and pastoral visiting. You represent Jesus. You are not a "society" man, nor a "club" man, but, like Elijah of old, a "man of God." "The King's business requires haste"; transact your business for God and souls, and move on. A minister's visits, nine times out of ten, relate to the souls, the spiritual welfare of his people. Gossiping and visiting after meeting is dismissed at night have often grieved the Holy Ghost, and ruined the service, and social visiting and chit chat after spiritual exercise undo all the work previously done in pastoral calls. Never lose sight of the fact that you are seeking the lost, comforting and instructing the saints; and nothing is unimportant, nothing costs too much, that will win a soul or lead it closer to God.

Let every preacher learn well the lesson—pay attention to the aged. It is especially due to them when they are the servants of the Lord Jesus Christ. "Inasmuch as ye have done it unto one of the least of these, ye have done it unto me." Many of them live in the past. They talk of the good times of long ago, and catch fire when they talk. Some time ago I was in Kentucky, on one of Dr. Godbey's first charges, and I was told that many old saints there, when relating their experience in witnessing for God, tell of their conversion "when Brother Godbey was on the work." One of the greatest sorrows of old age flows from neglect. The prayers of the aged saints are a benediction to the preacher. I cherish through the years the memory of a precious old saint, Sister Anderson, the mother of Mrs. Elizabeth Hoag, of Martin, Mich., who would meet me on Monday morning during the winter seasons, when she could not get out to services, and say, "Did you have a good time yesterday, Brother Kulp?" and upon being told of the services, she would say, "I knew you would, I was praying for you." She was eighty years of age, knew God, and knew how to prevail in prayer. We missed her when she went home.

Pay attention to children. Jesus did. You must. "Of such is the kingdom of heaven." "Except ye . . . become as little children, ye shall in no wise enter the kingdom." Aim to win them for God, and to retain them in the Church. Instruct them, help them to get settled, rooted, grounded, established, before they backslide. Half the effort made to retain them, would keep them. Said a young girl, "They leave us alone till we are fourteen, and then they bother the life out of us." Paul wrote to Timothy, "From a child thou hast known the Scriptures." A child five years old was asked, "How long have you been a Christian?" and he replied, "Ever since I was a little boy." And his mother affirms he was converted when he was two years old and was the best Christian in the house. Some time ago I read the obituary of a woman who passed on at one hundred and five years of age. She was converted when five years old, and lived a century for God. Someone cared for a child, and thus secured a hundred years of godly testimony. The preacher should help train the child in the way he should go. Claim the young for God, make it a business. We have hundreds of evangelists who are in the field and doing good work for God, but only one Payson Hammond. Bishop Quayle says, " 'Snug up to youth' is the advice of a wise pastor to his church, and is the wise advice to a pastor for himself. Youth for God is the world's safety. To start with God and stay with God, what a shelter from temptation, what a safe conduct on the long, grim way of life."

To start with God, we said—and we mean it. I wish every preacher would procure Dr. Godbey's book, just issued, on theology, and read there a Scriptural presentation of the truth regarding children. A recent author writes, "Only two theories are possible touching a child at his birth. Theory one: The child belongs to the devil. Theory two: The child belongs to God."* The church or the person who would rise and make a disquisition to prove that the child belongs to the devil would have a hazardous enterprise. The common sense of mankind knows better. When the common sense of mankind, and the view of Jesus are at one, we may allow that the coincident voices of Christ and humanity are always wise. Suppose we consider the first view, namely that the child is the devil's child. No man could get a hearing for a moment in championing such a theory. The other theory is that every child belongs to God, was born God's child, before he can belong to that wicked one and arrive at such unworthy notoriety. Across the path of every child thrusts out the jutting crag—"for of such is the kingdom of heaven." In the light of Jesus' authoritative and conclusive saying, we must frame our theories of the child as related to God; and the child as related to God is the measure of the child's relation to the Christian Church.

"Jesus Christ, by the grace of God, tasted death for every man," is the statement of universal redemption. In that sunlight we may walk swiftly and safely. There are no heathen children born into this world, all the babes born into this world are Christians. The world is born Christian. Every soul born among men is a saved soul. I consider this the greatest thought which has ever crossed the path of my

*Quayle "The Pastor-preacher."

thinking. It is sublime, heartening, illuminating. Children are born in heathen lands, but they are not heathen; they are Christians. There are only heathen men and women. There are sinners in the world, but there are no persons born sinners. Hear the Christ: "For of such is the kingdom of God." This is said of all babies. There is every sort of difference between being born "sinful" and being born "sinner." Everybody is born "sinful" "as the sparks fly upward," but to sinfulness there attaches no guilt. We are not responsible for a bent. To "sinnerness" there attaches guilt. "Sinfulness" and "sinnerness" are radically different terms. We are born sinful: we make ourselves sinners. To doubt that the babe dying is safely housed in Heaven would be strange atheism. "The streets of the city are full of boys and girls" is the laughter-laden description of the City of God given long since by a prophet who saw things as they were. You cannot listen for the heavenly song and not hear children singing. Children are born in the kingdom of Christ. This the preacher must not fail to know, and this the preacher must never forget, and if children belong to the kingdom of God, they belong to the Church of God, and have the right and privileges of the Church. "Forbid them not, for of such is the kingdom of God."

CHAPTER IX

The Preacher's Difficulties

"Elias was a man subject to like passions as we are, and he prayed." James wrote that line, and we can get much comfort from it. The Apostle who walked with our Lord and sat under His ministry associates himself and the church with the old prophet of a previous dispensation, in human infirmities. Ministers of today are much like ministers of previous days—just as weak, but no weaker; just as good, but no better. Say not the former days were better than these, for thou sayest not wisely—neither say the difficulties were greater. We today contend against the same allurements, same unbelief, "same worldliness, same forgetfulness of God, same tendencies to vanity, self-confidence, levity, moroseness, presumption, discouragement, envy, anger, resentment, duplicity, hardness of heart, uncharitableness," that have been found in all the past. Just as many false brethren, with the perils attendant, just as much care connected with the churches, just as many heart burnings and jealousies. The third chapter of Romans, ninth to the eighteenth verses, contains an indictment of human nature that is just as applicable to humanity today as when it was written. All the culture and education the world furnishes has not altered the carnal mind which is still enmity against God, and it is still true, "they that are in the flesh, and walk after the flesh, cannot please God." And all of these things are insistent in their opposition to godliness and impel the preacher to constant watchfulness and earnest prayer for the supply of the Spirit.

The world and the worldly church are not in love with holiness, with Bible salvation, or with full Gospel preachers. The preacher determined to go with God will find all Hell arranged against him, and in alliance with these worldly preachers, and worldly church-members. The more loyal he is to God, and the more faithful he is to his calling, the more he will be opposed. "Marvel not if the world hate you, it hated me before it hated you," Jesus said to His disciples. "Pick out the officers," is a rule with the devil when assailing the Church. Paul was "in labors more abundant," and as a consequence he was a shining mark for the fiery darts of the wicked one. A messenger of Satan was sent to buffet him that he might not be exalted above measure.

One of the preacher's difficulties lies in his temptation to be critical of his brethren in the ministry. Too often he "damns by faint praise." "It was a good sermon, but—" If one cannot find something in a brother preacher to appreciate, let him not depreciate. Dr. Quayle says, "Depreciation is a shallow man's gift." "Of all the follies which wise men commit, not one is more folly mad than that view which supposes that by how much some brother minister is praised, by that much one's self is dispraised, or that by how much a brother minister is held in slight esteem, by so much the greater esteem will come to one's self. The facts of experience give the lie to all such meanness as this." He is a small man who depreciates his brother. "We know we have passed from death unto life because we love the brethren" applies to preachers as well as laymen, and "love makes one appreciative." "To rejoice in another's success is both worthy a preacher's manliness and a good schooling for the heart." "Appreciation may be acquired, and blessed is the preacher who acquires it."

Another difficulty besetting the preacher is the temptation to boast of his own labors and the results, and it is all the more dangerous because of the numerous examples. There are few John Hatfields in the matter of writing reports. May his tribe increase and God be glorified thereby! We have grown weary of reports that told of "the greatest meeting the city ever saw." "Nothing like it in the remembrance of the oldest member." "The glory rolled and rolled, wave after wave of glory." "The whole country stirred for miles around." We call this temptation a difficulty because it is such a difficult matter for some to overcome it, but grace is free and we are prayerful and hopeful.

While the minister of the Gospel, called of God to preach, is "to speak as one that has authority," let him not play the part of boss. There are political bosses, and financial bosses, and family bosses, but the church boss is worse than all combined. "I am among you as the serving one" was the language and life of Him who left the glory that He had with the Father, to take upon Himself our nature and He should be our Example, and Exemplar. Authority, and especially spiritual authority, has been found to be a dangerous possession, and yet it belongs to the ministry. "Let no man despise thy youth," wrote Paul to a young minister. To another he wrote, "Those things speak, and exhort and rebuke with all authority. Let no man despise thee." Popes are not needed anywhere; much less, then, in the Holiness Movement. Clothed with a little brief authority, men strut for their hour, puffed by love of place and the flatteries of place-seeking men and wily women. Paul, hard-headed old logician that he was, saw the danger, and said, "Put not a novice into the ministry, lest being puffed up with pride, he fall into the condemnation of the devil." Men who are called good, and are good, have often been puffed up when they ought to have been humbled in the dust. There never comes a time when a minister should fail "to walk softly before the Lord." The man in the pulpit should have convictions of his own, born of study of the Word, guidance of the Spirit, and communion with God, yet he should always be the pastor, the brother, the friend, the counsellor, but never the boss.

Another difficulty in the ministry is discouragement, and of all the lean, blue demons Hell ever launched against the ministry, this is one of the meanest. The man of God has a right to look for results, but oftentimes he will find prejudice, ignorance, and indifference, to which are added pleasure-seeking and worldly prosperity, confronting him like a wall of adamant. We say worldly prosperity for the worldling of this hour is prosperity mad, and the great revivals of the past have often been in times of adversity. Men will act as though they cared nothing for these things, church-members will be full of carnality and averse to prayer and fasting, waiting before God in a devotional spirit. Good people around will be disheartened by the indifference and formality and say effort is useless. Then is the time for the preacher to "encourage himself in the Lord"; to cry out and shout, for great is the Holy One of Israel in the midst of Zion. While looking at his surroundings, he may be tempted to say, "Who is sufficient for these things?" Let him "look up," until he learns "our sufficiency is of God." A valley of dry bones may be soon teeming with Spirit-born men and women, living witnesses to the power of God. Our God is faithful, and the man called to preach will have a measure of success that will make God glad and Heaven rejoice over souls won by the power of the Gospel.

Chapter X

The Preacher's Reward

There is a present reward to every man of God called to preach, and that is a consciousness of the privilege of preaching the Gospel. "The tongue's holiest mission is to proclaim the Christ." Standing as an ambassador of the King of kings, between God and men, knowing he has a message and burning in soul until it is delivered, angels, if capable of envy, might envy him. He is not only a preacher, he is a witness: "that which we have seen and heard declare we unto you."

"What we have felt and seen
With confidence we tell,
And publish to the sons of men,
The signs infallible."

Having "tested, and tried it, and proved it, he knows God's promise is true," and "knowing that he knows," he treads like a giant and proclaims boldly his God-given truths. "The preacher is the man Christ left to say His words to men. He is to say the thing Christ would say if he were here." Is this not a privilege? Carnegie gave ten million dollars for a Peace Foundation, and already there is a host of applicants who want to go hither and thither proclaiming disarmament among the nations, peace on earth, and war no more. JESUS left an unfinished work, and trusted men and women called of God, to push the battle. "GO YE" is the command, and with it comes the enabling, aye, more, the very presence of the Commander. The person realizing this will realize a present reward. He will be so in earnest his message will have him. He will know as did that man from the wilderness, "I am the Voice," a voice from Heaven. "As though God did beseech you by us, we beseech you in Christ's stead." Privilege? Aye, the greatest human beings could have, to stand in His stead, give His message, persuading men to be reconciled unto God. Following in the footsteps of the Man of

Galilee, seeking to save the lost, and preaching that which prophets failed to apprehend, and angels desired to look into; I pity the man who does not know this is the greatest privilege Heaven could bestow. The men who talk of their "sacrifices" and "what they gave up to enter the ministry," advertise their ignorance of the preacher's present reward, and their unfitness for this work.

If "it is more blessed to give than to receive"—and no man who has the Spirit of Christ questions this—then it is a privilege to HELP those around us. If the woman rejoiced over the lost piece of money found, if the shepherd rejoiced over the lost sheep brought back to the fold, if the father rejoiced, was merry and glad, because the prodigal came back home, then we ought to esteem it a privilege to help the lost ones back to God, and rejoice in the privilege of finding them for Jesus' sake.

I think I had a foretaste of that which gladdens the heart of Jesus, once, as I stood by a death bed. Esther Nichols was passing away, leaving for home. Disease had done its work in emaciating the form, and sapping the strength, but the mind was clear as ever. The end was not far off, as she turned her great, black eyes toward me and said, "Oh, you have helped me so often." My heart was filled with gratitude to God and my eyes with tears, that I had had the privilege of being helpful to one of God's chosen ones.

Falling From Grace

26 Reasons Why the Possibility of Apostasy Is Taught in the Word of God

By

Rev. C. F. Wimberly, B.A., D.D.

Falling From Grace

There are a number of terms by which this doctrine and its antitheses are known: Apostasy, Final Perseverance, Once in Grace Always in Grace, etc. These expressions are theological terms, and are also familiar even among the common people. The doctrine is one of the vital points around which Arminianism and Calvinism have fought for centuries. Calvinism says, once the soul is converted, regenerated, adopted into the family of God, through Grace, that this relation can never be forfeited; as it is retained through the power and majesty of Grace, and is not predicated upon conduct, good or bad. In order that the reader may get a clear statement of this doctrine firsthand, and not by hearsay, we quote an extract from a sermon, delivered before a state gathering, of a church which makes this tenet prominent in all their public deliverances.

"Good works cannot save a man nor damn a soul," he said. "He that believeth on the Son, whatever else he does or does not, has everlasting life and never will be lost. Two men, one a sinner, the other a Christian, may commit a wrong and get killed. The one dies and goes to hell; the other goes to heaven. The Christian loses only his reward, for his life was hid in Christ Jesus and could not be plucked from him. Our character, conduct or life has nothing to do with our salvation. The saved man will want to do right and if he unwittingly falls into sin, he will repent of it, but that has nothing to do with salvation. 'I say unto you that he that believeth on him hath everlasting life.' There is no judgment for the Christian; only judgment is for the sinner. The very moment I believe, all the judgment for my sin is transferred from the future to the past and there is no judgment for me."

Once in Grace, always in Grace," is one of the shibboleths of ultra Calvinism. Arminianism says that sonship sustains the relation of a covenant, and, as such, can stand only as both parties keep the covenant inviolate; that a son of God, through the New Birth, may experience all the blessings of the Atonement, even that of purity of heart; then forfeit it all through transgression. Apostasy and Falling from Grace are synonymous terms and are used interchangeably.

Just how such an interpretation could have become so prominent in religious polemics is hard to understand, but it towers up as one of the big fundamentals of Calvinism. The theological war between these two branches of teaching has been long and bitter. But of the "Five Points" of difference, all but this one have gone down before the Gibraltar logic of Arminianism. This one still remains, unabashed, bold, vociferous, even in the face of unequivocal statements from the Word of God, in the face of observation, and human experience.

The writer was in conversation with an ardent advocate of this very wholesome doctrine; whereupon, this presumptuous enthusiast declared: "I *know* that I am as sure of heaven, as if I were there. I have been converted, and I don't care what I may, or may not do—even murder—I am sustained by Grace and not by my own effort or will." To this hilarious speech, I replied: "My brother, I will give you $100 if you will find me one Scripture which teaches what you have just said, beyond a shadow of a doubt; one that teaches it so clearly that I can see it. I shall be delighted to pay over that amount of money for the assurance it would give me. I want a 'thus saith the Lord' and you can get the money." It is needless to say that the money was not called for.

We do not hesitate to say, with all sincerity, and in the fear of God, that this doctrine is utterly without Scriptural foundation, and harmful in the extreme, just as any other perversion of God's word is harmful. We are persuaded that the continual emphasis placed upon this teaching by ministers of the Gospel has done incalculable harm. In the subsequent pages we propose to give twenty-six reasons why the Possibility of Apostasy—or falling from Grace as a possibility—is sustained in the Bible. We hear the sarcastic remark: "Why, they believe in falling from Grace." We deny this absolutely; we do not believe in falling from Grace, but we believe in the possibility. Transgression is just as sure to be punished or pardoned, as God's government is established in justice and righteousness; "the soul that sinneth, it shall die."

We therefore offer the following reasons for the faith that is within us:

1. Men are not machines—they are personalities; free to act and think as they choose. All the rewards and punishments—in this life, and in the life to come—are vitally connected with the doctrine of Free Moral Agency—Free Intellectual Agency, as well. Men are undoubtedly free; and if they are not—then, the whole system of human divine government is wrong and should be revised. If they are free at any time, they are free all the time; they are accountable at any time, they are accountable at all times. If the wrath of God rests on men at any time, on account of sin, then it must, of necessity and justice, rest on them at all times. Transgression of a law at one time, is the same in character, as at any other time. Adultery after conversion is the same in character as before conversion; theft does not change in character, because the thief has once known God. By what hocus-pocus conjuring may a sin be culpable before conversion, and then be free from condemnation after conversion? If sin after conversion does not produce guilt—then Free Agency is destroyed. The two propositions are at extremes, and cannot be reconciled by any sane law of reasoning; it does not require logic to see the absurdity of such a plea—all that is required—just common sense. If men are free—their acts are the result of free choice. If men cannot forfeit their relation with God by sin, it can only be so because responsibility is not involved.

2. If "once in grace, always in grace," is the Bible teaching, and if the truly regenerated cannot be lost, then God's attitude to sin, must of necessity, be changed. All must agree that sin defiles the soul before conversion; then the defilement is actually greater after conversion, as their spiritual eyes are open to the nature of sin, in a manner not possible before. If sin after conversion does not forfeit the relation of sonship; then God's attitude to sin is changed. This would destroy the Immutability of God. His attitude to sin must ever remain the same; else He is a changeable Being. God is holy; God is justice, and when He palliates and winks at men's transgressions—committed in anger—lust—or covetousness—He is no longer the Immutable God, which the Bible emphatically teaches us that He is.

3. If we teach the doctrine; "once in grace, always in

grace"—that those in grace are no longer under the law, but under grace; and this law of unqualified mercy is the law to which they are amenable, *the standard of life of necessity* is lowered. The ideals of Christian character tumble far below the standard set up by the world—not to mention the standard taught in the Word of God. "He that saith he abideth in him, ought himself, also, to walk even as he walked."

That scripture places the standard on a high and holy plane—even that which was occupied by the Master Himself. "He that abideth in him, sinneth not," says John. From Genesis to Revelation, there is an eternal condemnation and denunciation of sin, anywhere; the standard is not lowered by divine authority; transgression of law escapes the penalty nowhere. God even spared not His angels that kept not their first estate; then He will surely not spare His enlightened children, who know better. When we teach to the contrary, the standard of living is lowered; hence the doctrine is wrong—false—and contradicts the whole sweep of Bible teachings.

4. If sin after conversion does not involve guilt, therefore, not punishable, then *God is a respecter of persons.* Sin before conversion renders us guilty and punishable; one sin unpardoned and unpunished would wreck the moral government of God. If sin is so bitterly condemned at one period of a free moral agent's life, and condoned at another, God is a respecter of persons and partial. The Bible most emphatically teaches that He is not. Sin is sin, anywhere, and the supposed difference of character, by whom it is committed, does not change the polluting effects. By what law, or by what system of ethics or justice, shall it be punished in the sinner and go unpunished, when committed by those who profess to follow the One who came to save us from sin?

5. If converted men can commit sin at all, and not lose their standing before God; then they can commit any sin in the Decalogue: murder, adultery, arson, etc. If this is a Bible doctrine, it should be heralded from the housetops—and indeed, it is being done in some circles; but what of the consequences: every door of temptation is wide-open to all of God's people. If one Christian can sin, and remain in God's favor, then all of them may do the same. If a pastor of a church should be guilty of gross immorality, and this gospel was

reached by him, and believed by his parishioners, they must not cast him out, to be consistent. He would have a perfect right to demand that they leave him unmolested as their spiritual shepherd. Dear reader, the suggestion of such a thing is revolting. Sin is so subtle, and so alluring, that every door of temptation should be closed and locked; the stay-chains of our moral power are sure to break, if in the face of a fierce temptation, we believe there will be no condemnation before God. Away with such religious poison!

6. The doctrine of Impossibility of Apostasy places a false, unreasonable, and an unscriptural meaning to benefits of Grace; a meaning which cannot be sustained by a single passage in the Word of God, if reasonably interpreted. To say that God's children can no longer be judged by the law, but by Grace, gives it a meaning which is strained and distorted. By grace we are saved—but it is through faith, and faith must be preceded by repentance. The sinner: guilty, lost, undone—seeks pardon, and gets it; that is Grace—unmerited favor. This grace, acting in *exactly the same way,* continues to abound to usward. That is the "Amazing grace, how sweet the sound," of which we sing; but we have no right or authority to place such an extravagant meaning on grace, that it will palliate and condone sin. It is unreasonable, unscriptural —false!

7. Impossibility of Apostasy is unquestionably the most dangerous doctrine taught and believed by the followers of Jesus Christ. Purgatory, priestly absolution, masses for the dead—the grossest dogmas of Rome, are not to be compared with it. Rome's dogmas are too absurd for consideration by spiritually enlightened people; but this doctrine has a luscious, toothsome fascination about it, that hides the *hemlock* in the glass of nectar. Three reasons why it is dangerous: 1. It flatly contradicts the Word of God: "The soul that sinneth, it shall surely die," rings out clear and strong from almost every page in Holy Writ. 2. It sets at naught the spirit of careful, prayerful watchfulness—so forcibly enjoined upon us by the Master. It takes away the necessity for watchfulness; there is no danger, or risk in hot watching. 3. It restrains the impulse to repent deeply and pungently, after a sin has been committed. Why repent? There is no law broken—it is the law of grace. Hence, multitudes may become hopelessly backslidden by holding to this dangerous heresy.

8. "Once in grace, always in grace," does violence to reason and common sense. While our religion is one of faith, there is no feature of it that does not appeal to the soundest reason and common sense. All the warnings and commands in the Bible are based upon the highest system of ethics and justice known to man. When we examine this doctrine in the light of the whole teaching of the Bible; and viewed from every reasonable angle, whereby an observation can be made, it sweeps away reason and common sense, and should be rejected.

9. If those who sin after conversion are immune from the condemnation of God and the penalties which the same sin would entail upon others—the true ethics of rewards and punishments are destroyed. A reward—if one at all—is for the merit only. Rewards, promotions, and praise, that are not predicated on true merit—merit that has been justly demonstrated—is not merit at all—but *favoritism?* Let us illustrate: a father is the teacher of pupils in school; among the students are his own children. This man has certain rules which he has established for the government and discipline of the school; these rules must be obeyed; any violation entails punishment, and the teacher rigidly enforces this administration. Finally, one of his own children breaks the rules, with every feature of wilful disobedience. What happens? The father very graciously suspends the penalty, and the child goes unpunished. Such a procedure would provoke universal disapprobation from the public—parents of the other children; and it would result in a revolt among the pupils—and justly so. In like manner God cannot pass over the wilful sins of His children. If one can go unpunished; then the vilest may, and the principles or rewards and punishments are flagrantly set aside.

10. If it is true, that Christians may sin, and do so without losing their standing with God; there must of necessity be a weakness, somewhere in the Atonement, or a violent disregard for its efficacy. We reject it utterly from the standpoint of the Atonement—as it renders the ultimate and uttermost power of the Blood as useless and unnecessary. Why have a Saviour at all? Why have an Atonement—if it cannot save us from sin; and it does not matter whether the delivery from sin is complete or not? He came to destroy the works of the devil, and to save His people *from* their sins.

If, after they are saved—they continue in sin, the ultimate and uttermost power of the Blood is unnecessary. Why should He make intercession for us, if it is not to keep us from falling? Such a doctrine is a burning libel on the Blood of Jesus Christ, which John says, cleanseth from all sin.

11. If sin of any character, committed by anyone, under any circumstances, can remain without pardon or punishment—and that is what happens, if converted people can sin without condemnation; then the moral and righteous government of God breaks down. Sin cannot be committed without defilement; then defiled souls may enter heaven, which would also wreck God's throne. Arminianism believes that when converted people commit sin, they must do their first works over by repentance and faith, before they can be restored to divine favor again.

12. We are taught in the Word, that God's relation with men is that of a Covenant; it was so from the beginning, and has not changed today. God called it a "Covenant keeping God," and as such, there are at least two parties involved; it would not be a Covenant if one party assumed all the obligations. The Old Testament should read "The Old Covenant," and the "New Covenant" for the New Testament. When godly people broke their part of the Old Covenant they became the slaves and servants of the enemy. We have never found a single exception to this, until they had repented, and God came to their rescue. Our relation to God has never ceased to be a Covenant; any other view is nothing less than absurd.

13. Those who hold to this doctrine are forced by consistency, in order to be within reason and logic, to one of two conclusions. (a) That sin may be committed and remain unpardoned; or (b) that when a Christian sins, it is the body, and not the soul involved by the transgression. Sin remains only in the body, and the soul is not defiled. The first horn of the dilemma, as stated before, destroys God's righteous government; the second is the old First Century Gnosticism out on twentieth century dress parade; the last one is physiologically, psychologically, biologically, theologically, and judicially false.

14. We will now take up a few examples. Thus far we have been discussing this from the standpoint of reason, and

have said but little touching Bible proofs. We will confine the remainder of this question to the Bible teachings. Our first example is King Saul. God called this big, humble young man to be king over His people; and after he was anointed, God gave him a new heart (1 Sam. 10:9) and honored him in every way. We shall not follow up the history of Saul; but he became a transgressor, and confesses that "God hears me no more" (1 Sam. 28:15).

We find in another place where the Spirit of the Lord departed from Saul, and an evil spirit came upon him (1 Sam. 16:14). Here was a man whom God had changed and blessed; then afterwards, the Lord leaves him because of sin. On the night before he committed suicide, this man, who once was the humble servant of God, goes down into a cave and listens to the cantillations of an old hag; and again confesses that God had departed from him. 1 Sam. 28:15-20. Here is an unmistakable case of apostasy.

15. We notice in the next place, the case of Amaziah. He also was a king under the direction of God, and ruling in righteousness; but the Book says he turned away from the Lord, and worshipped the god of Seir. Whereupon, the wrath of God was kindled against him, ending in his destruction (2 Chron. 25:14, 15, 27). We ask the reader to examine these references, and verify the statements herein set forth. We are taking the simple records of the Bible; these mean something, or nothing.

16. We now come to the example of Judas. He was chosen of the Master to have an honored place in the Apostolic College; the Master ordained him to preach the kingdom of God, and peform miracles. He did both. The Master told them all, at one time, that their names were written in heaven (Luke 10:20). Two times it was recorded—or rather, two of the gospels say, that Satan entered the heart of Judas (Luke 22:3, John 13:27). Now, they tell us that Judas was a devil from the beginning; but how could this be? For Satan would have been in all the time; the above references prove that he was not a devil. Jesus knew men's hearts, and to say that He selected, ordained, and commissioned a devil to preach, is an insult to the Son of God. But, listen, we are told that from this ministry and apostleship, Judas fell, through transgression. See Acts 1:25. This puts an end to all the argu-

ments, so far as Judas is concerned. Another clear case of Apostasy.

17. Then, there is the example of Hymenaeus and Alexander. Of these characters we know nothing, except Paul's brief statement. He had been exhorting Timothy to war a good warfare; holding on to the faith, not as some who had failed to do so, and had made shipwreck of themselves. He then mentions these two parties as having done the very thing he warns Timothy not to do. They once had the faith, and a good conscience, but let them go for the pleasures of this present world. Paul said he had turned them over to Satan. 1 Tim. 1:18-20.

18. We shall now take up the testimony of the various writers of the Bible. We will begin with Isaiah, the greatest of the major prophets. We find in the first chapter a strong exhortation for the people who had gone away from the Lord to return, and He would restore them. "Though your sins be as scarlet, they shall be white as snow; though they be red like crimson they shall be as wool." All through Isaiah, the wonderful promises are conditional; the conditions were: They must return unto serving Him, and keep His commandments; not one promise, but is based upon a condition. He declares that Israel shall be restored with judgment, and not grace. Hear Isaiah's testimony, relative to this doctrine: "And they that forsake the Lord shall be consumed" Isa. 1:28. This could not have meant the heathen, for they had never been followers of the Lord.

19. *Ezekiel's Testimony.* Nothing in all the Bible is so clear-cut and conclusive. We give three references. "Again, when a righteous man doth turn from his righteousness, and commit iniquity, and I lay a stumblingblock before him, he shall die: because thou hast not given him warning, he shall die in his sin, and his righteousness which he hath done shall not be remembered; but his blood which I will require at thy hand" Ezek. 3:20.

"But when the righteous turneth away from his righteousness and committeth iniquity, and doeth according to all the abominations that the wicked man doeth, shall he live? All his righteousness that he hath done shall not be mentioned: in his trespass that he hath trespassed, and in his sin that he hath sinned, in them shall he die" Ezek. 18:24.

"Therefore, thou son of man, say to the children of thy people, The righteousness of the righteous shall not deliver him in the day of his transgression. . . . neither shall the righteous be able to live for his righteousness in the day that he sinneth" Ezek. 33:12. "But," says one, "this is the Old Testament—that was under the law; we are now under Grace." But Jesus said that not "One jot or tittle of His word should pass away, until it was fulfilled," or exemplified. God could not afford to be more severe with His people then, with little light, than now, with more light.

20. *The testimony of Jesus.* "When the unclean spirit is gone out of a man he walketh in dry places, seeking rest; and finding none, he saith, I will return to my house whence I came out. And when he cometh, he findeth it swept and garnished. Then goeth he and taketh to him seven other spirits more wicked than himself; and they enter in and dwell there: and the last state of that man is worse than the first" Luke 11:24-26.

"They on the rock are they, which when they hear receive the word with joy; and these have no root, which for a while they believe, but in the time of temptation fall away" Luke 8:13. The Master had but little to say, but what He did say cannot be gainsaid.

21. *The Testimony of John.* "From that time many of his disciples went back, and walked no more with him" John 6:66. 1 John 3:15 says very plainly, "that no murderer hath eternal life abiding in him." Now, if any sin which a man might commit, does not forfeit his standing with God, no sin will do it—even murder; but John says, that if he murders, even in his mind—in hate—eternal life does not abide in him. The thought is, that he might have had eternal life, but it will not abide where there is the spirit of murder. John says again: "Whosoever abideth in him, sinneth not" 1 John 3:6. To remain in grace, we cannot commit sin; when a sin is committed, or if we should sin—we at once sin out, until we repent and put that sin under the blood. We must agree with John, that to remain in grace, no sin can be committed. But, thank God, there is a wonderful provision: "if we sin, we have an advocate with the Father, Jesus Christ, the righteous." We must take one or the other of these propositions, or else rule out John's testimony. We prefer to believe John.

22. *The Testimony of Peter.* "For if these things be in you and abound, they make you that ye shall neither be barren, nor unfruitful in the knowledge of our Lord Jesus Christ. But he that lacketh these things is blind, and cannot see afar off, and hath forgotten that he was purged from his old sins. Wherefore, the rather, brethren, give diligence to make your calling and election sure; for if ye do these things *ye shall never fall*: for so an entrance shall be ministered unto you abundantly into the everlasting kingdom of our Lord and Saviour Jesus Christ" II Peter 1:8-11. Once more: "Ye therefore, beloved, seeing ye know these things before, beware lest ye also, being led away with the error of the wicked, fall from your own stedfastness" II Peter 3:17. These clear statements need no comment; the words themselves give all the strength necessary to substantiate the truth of our contention, and the fallacy of our good friends who take the opposite view.

23. *The Testimony of Jude.* "I will therefore, put you in remembrance, though ye once knew this, how that the Lord, having saved the people out of the land of Egypt, afterwards destroyed them that believed not. And the angels which kept not their first estate, but left their own habitation, he hath reserved in everlasting chains under darkness unto the judgment of the great day" Jude 5, 6. "Now unto him that is able to keep you from falling, and to present you faultless before the presence of his glory with exceeding joy" Jude 24. Here are three straight-edges on this subject; each one clinches the proposition, as much as language can do it. He is able to keep us from falling; but why put such a promise there, if there were no danger of falling? The bugle clarion is loud and clear, that if we sin, after knowing God, we forfeit our standing before Him, until we repent.

24. *The Testimony of Hebrews.* "Take heed, brethren, lest there be in any of you an evil heart of unbelief, in departing from the living God. But exhort one another daily, while it is called today, lest any of you be hardened through the deceitfulness of sin. For we are made partakers of Christ, if we hold the beginning of our confidence *stedfast unto the end*" Heb. 3:12-24. "For it is impossible for those who were once enlightened, and have tasted of the heavenly gift, and were made partakers of the Holy Ghost, and have tasted of the good word of God and the powers of the world to come,

If they fall away, to renew them again unto repentance, seeing they crucify to themselves the Son of God afresh, and put him to an open shame" Heb. 6:4-6. "For if we sin wilfully, after that we have received the knowledge of the truth, there remaineth no more sacrifice for sins, but a certain looking for of judgment and fiery indignation, which shall devour the adversaries." A better rendering of this last reference, is that if we continue "to sin on and on, wilfully," etc., we may repent of our sins, for a while; but we reach a place, where there will be no chance for us even to repent. All these teach us that there is no such thing as a corner on grace; whatever we do, we must do it *unto the end.* Besides the above, there are a number of places in Hebrews, where the word *lest* is used, each one of them which is most significant; do certain things—*lest* something befall us. "Lest we let them slip," "Lest we come short," etc. These are so plain, that a wayfaring man, though a fool, need not err therein.

25. *The Testimony of Paul.* We have left the old War Horse of the Gospel to last, except that of Revelation, which should be our closing proofs. We will give three statements from Paul. "I keep under my body, and bring it into subjection: lest that by any means, when I have preached to others, I myself should be a castaway" 1 Cor. 9:27. "Now the Spirit speaketh expressly, that in the latter times some shall depart from the faith, giving heed to seducing spirits, and doctrines of devils" 1 Tim. 4:1. "I have fought a good fight, I have finished my course, I have kept the faith: henceforth there is laid up for me a crown of righteousness, which the Lord, the righteous judge shall give me at that day: and not to me only, but unto them also that love his appearing" 2 Tim. 4:7, 8. Paul predicted his receiving the crown at the last day, upon the fact that he *fought,* and *kept,* and *finished*; thus it will be with us all.

26. *The Testimony of Revelation.* "Nevertheless I have somewhat against thee, because thou hast left thy first love. Remember therefore from whence thou art fallen, and repent, and do thy first works else I will come unto thee quickly, and will remove thy candlestick out of his place, except thou repent" Rev. 2:4, 5. Hear this remarkable text: "Behold, I come quickly: hold fast that which thou hast, that no man take thy crown." Crowns are laid up for us, after we have

done as Paul—fought, kept, and finished; then there will be a chance, that our crown may be given to another. Again: "He that overcometh, the same shall be clothed in white raiment; and I will not blot his name out of the book of life; but I will confess his name before my Father, and before his angels" Rev. 3:5. Then, the Laodiceans were told that because of their lukewarmness, neither hot nor cold, that He would spew them out of His mouth, because they were unfit for use of any kind. Rev. 3:15, 16. This was spoken to a church; a church that had grown cold and indifferent, and the Spirit warns this church of the sure destiny awaiting it, because it had forsaken the Lord, and had become proud and rich. Where could a more severe utterance be found, than to be spewed out of His mouth? What remains for us to do, in the face of such overwhelming testimony and reason? First, we must abandon this dangerous doctrine, and pray without ceasing, in the fight that is before us. "Seeing we are encompassed about with so great a cloud of witnesses, let us run with patience the race that is set before us—looking unto Jesus, the author and the finisher of our faith."